Wild Animals

GORILLA

 Lionel Bender

Chrysalis Children's Books

First published in the UK in 2004 by
Chrysalis Children's Books
An imprint of Chrysalis Books Group Plc,
The Chrysalis Building, Bramley Road,
London W10 6SP

ISBN 1 84458 169 1

British Library Cataloguing in Publication Data
for this book is available from the British Library.

Editorial Manager *Joyce Bentley*
Senior Editor *Rasha Elsaeed*
Editorial Assistant *Camilla Lloyd*

Produced by Bender Richardson White
Project Editor *Lionel Bender*
Designer *Ben White*
Production *Kim Richardson*
Picture Researcher *Cathy Stastny*
Cover Make-up *Mike Pilley, Radius*

Printed in China

10 9 8 7 6 5 4 3 2 1

Words in **Bold** can be found in New words on page 31.

Typography *Natascha Frensch*
Read Regular, READ SMALLCAPS and Read Space; European Community Design Registration 2003
and Copyright © Natascha Frensch 2001-2004 **Read Medium**, **Read Black** and *Read Slanted*
Copyright © Natascha Frensch 2003-2004

READ™ is a revolutionary new typeface that will enchance children's understanding through clear, easily
recognisable character shapes. With its evenly spaced and carefully designed characters, READ™ will help
children at all stages to improve their literacy skills, and is ideal for young readers, reluctant readers and
especially children with dyslexia.

Picture credits
Cover © Digital Vision. © Digital Vision pages 1, 2, 4, 9, 10, 12, 13, 16, 17, 18, 19, 21, 23, 24, 25. © Corbis Images Inc.:
pages 17 (Paul A. Sauders), 24 (Rob C. Nunnington/Gallo Images), 27 (Kevin Schafer/Corbis, 29 (Reuters/Corbis Images).
© Frank Lane Picture Agency Limited: pages 5 (Mark Newman), 6 (E. & O. Hosking), 8 (Phil Ward), 14 (Frank Lanting/Minden
Pictures), 15 (Silvestris Fotoservice), 20 (Silvestris Fotoservice), 22 (Silvestris Fotoservice), 26 (C. Ellis/Minden Pictures), 28
(Silvestris Fotoservice), 29 (P. Ward). © RSPCA Photolibrary: pages 7 (Andrew Routh), 11 (Alyson Pearce).

Contents

Big gorillas

Gorillas are much like humans and chimpanzees but bigger.

They can grow to 1.9 m tall and weigh 200 kg. A gorilla can live for up to 30 years.

Homes

Gorillas live in **rainforests** in the middle of Africa.

Some gorillas live on **lowlands**, where it is warm. Others live in cool areas in the mountains.

Food

The gorilla eats mostly plants.
Its favourite foods are leaves
and stems.

A gorilla also eats fruit, ferns and nettles. If it is very hungry, it will eat snails and slugs.

Among the trees

A gorilla walks about 1 km a day to find food. It spends most of its time resting and eating.

Each evening, a gorilla makes a **nest** in the trees. Here it sleeps.

Living together

Gorillas live in groups. The biggest male is the leader in each group.

An **adult** male gorilla is bigger
and stronger than an adult female.
It also has more hair.

Senses

The gorilla has good hearing, eyesight and **sense** of smell.

It touches things and picks them up with its hands.

Defences

An adult gorilla is so big that few animals dare to threaten it.

Male gorillas have four big, pointed teeth. They use them in fights and to scare off enemies.

Skin and fur

The gorilla has tough skin. The skin is covered in **fur**.

Gorillas clean each other's fur.
They pick out dirt and insects
with their fingers.

Family life

A mother gorilla has one baby at a time. She feeds it on her milk until it is eight months old.

The baby is looked after by older gorillas in its family.

Growing up

The young gorilla learns to feed, make nests and climb trees.

Young gorillas stay close to their mothers until they are two years old.

Becoming an adult

Male gorillas are adult at age 15. Females are adult at age seven or eight years.

Young adult males leave their groups and live alone. Later they are joined by adult females.

In danger

Farmers are cutting down forests to make fields. They are destroying the gorillas' home.

Some people kill gorillas for their meat. Their **skulls** and skins may be sold as gifts.

Gorilla care

Scientists study gorillas in the wild to find out how to help the animals survive.

Young gorillas are looked after and their homes made into safe wildlife areas.

Quiz

1 How big do gorillas grow?

2 Where do gorillas live?

3 What do gorillas eat?

4 Where do gorillas sleep at night?

5 How long does a mother gorilla feed
her baby with her milk?

6 At what age do young gorillas start to go off
on their own?

7 Which are bigger – adult male or adult female gorillas?

8 Why do some people kill gorillas?

The answers are all in this book!

New words

adult fully grown and able to make babies.

fur thick hair that covers most of the body.

lowlands large area of generally flat land surrounding hills and mountains.

nest sort of bed or home made by an animal.

rainforests areas of trees that get lots of rain all year round. Most rainforests are in the middle of South America, Africa and South-east Asia.

sense the way animals find out about their surroundings. Animals have five senses – sight, hearing, smell, taste and touch. The body senses something when it notices it is there.

skull skeleton, or bony structure, of the head.

Index